The Tree of Life

God's Promise of Salvation

CONCORDIA PUBLISHING HOUSE · SAINT LOUIS

Table of Contents

Introduction

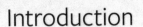

This book for The Tree of Life series is written to help give you an overview of God's vast, epic plan of salvation. It is divided into ten sections, or weeks, with each week having five readings. In all, there are fifty readings that help lead you through the high points of the overarching narrative that runs through the Bible. The first five sections give an overview of the Old Testament narrative. These show us what happened from the beginning of time to the coming of Jesus and focus on God's promises to send a Savior during those millennia. The second five sections focus on the New Testament narrative, especially the life, ministry, death, and resurrection of Jesus. The final week narrows in on Jesus' return, or Judgment Day. Each day also has a Bible verse and a reflection to help direct your thinking on what the narrative of God's plan of salvation means for you.

Use this as part of a congregational study on The Tree of Life series or on its own. We pray that you will be encouraged, blessed, and empowered to rejoice in God's great plan of salvation in Jesus for you, and that you faithfully and joyfully live out your days as God's redeemed child as you await the return of Jesus.

The Beginning of Our Story

DAY 1: CREATION

In the beginning, God created the heavens and the earth. (GENESIS 1:1)

We begin our journey through God's great plan of salvation at the beginning of all things. In Genesis 1, the first chapter of the first book of the Bible, we get a picture of God creating our reality. He started with the world and moved to the stars and finally to people. He did this solely by His Word, and as He spoke, things came into being. First, He created light, then space on earth, differentiating land from sea, ordering all things by His grand design. He created the stars, opening humanity's eyes to His wonders beyond our earth. He filled the land with vegetation, the sea with creatures, the sky with birds, and the land with animals. At the pinnacle of creation, God made the first man. God formed him out of the earth, much like a potter forming clay, then breathed life into him. Humans were special, formed in God's image, which means that the first man was made to serve God's purposes in His creation. Mankind was and is to serve God's creation, care for it, love it, develop it, and cherish it.

The creation account in Genesis is perhaps briefer than our imaginations would like, but in it God provides enough. In six natural days, God created all things, and on the seventh day He rested. Each day He created something new and wonderful, and in so doing created a rhythm and order to days and weeks for mankind to follow. This creation and this order were not to be static for humans but instead dynamic. We were not made to be idle but to find joy in our work and fulfillment in living out our God-given roles in relationship with Him, one another, and all of creation. Mankind was not made to fight for survival but to live in peace with God and creation, with no knowledge of sin or death but in endless contentment and fellowship with all creation forever. This reality is no longer ours since sin and death entered the world, but we look forward to the day when creation is restored for us in Jesus. We pray, come, Lord Jesus, come!

REFLECTION: Imagine what it would be like if there were no sin, death, or struggle for survival in your life and work. How would this transform your work for the better?

DAY 2: GOD CREATES ADAM AND EVE

Then the LORD God said, "It is not good that the man should be alone; I will make him a helper fit for him." (GENESIS 2:18)

After the grand creation account, the Bible moves to a more personal and intimate facet: the creation of man and woman. On the sixth day, God formed the first man from the earth and breathed into him the breath of life. He placed Adam (meaning "the man") in the Garden of Eden and gave him tasks. He was to work the ground, not eat of the forbidden tree, and name the creatures. As Adam named the creatures, he saw none like him. He was the special creation of God, made in God's image, yet Adam was not meant to be alone. God put Adam into a deep sleep, took a rib from his side, and formed the first woman, Eve. When Adam awoke, he marveled at Eve. He was no longer alone. God united Adam and Eve in marriage.

God created this model for marriage in His order before the world was corrupted by sin and death. It is no accident in Scripture that the creation of Adam and Eve has a special place at the end of the creation account. In it we see the building blocks of all human society by God's order and command. As men and women marry and have families of their own, God's design is for each child to be loved, cherished, protected, and taught as God adds his or her individual talents, gifts, and personality to the human family. In a very real way, the whole human race is an extension of that first family, played out over generations. Since sin and death came into the world, this perfect picture of marriage, relationships, fellowship, and ordered society has been corrupted. No family fully functions as God designed. Yet in Christ, there is forgiveness of sins and reconciliation. Those whom Jesus has called to be His are part of an even greater extended family of faith, one that will be finally realized and seen when He returns to make all things new.

REFLECTION: What are things that you can do in your own life today that help support and serve your immediate family and your extended church family? How might these things reflect God's love and care to others, as God originally intended for society?

DAY 3: THE FALL AND GOD'S FIRST PROMISE

> [God said,] "I will put enmity between you and the woman,
>   and between your offspring and her offspring;
> He shall bruise your head,
>   and you shall bruise His heel." (GENESIS 3:15)

God created the world in order and then man and woman to care for it. He had done this all in His design, making things "very good." This perfect world, with meaningful work and eternal life with God, creation, and one another, would not last.

In the Garden of Eden, God had planted two special trees. One was the tree of life; the other was the tree of the knowledge of good and evil. Eating of the tree of life, which God commanded them to do, would mean eternal life in paradise. The only thing God explicitly told Adam and Eve they could not do was eat from the tree of the knowledge of good and evil. The command seemed so simple, yet it would not be.

Satan, a fallen angel who had rebelled against God, came to Eve one day in the form of a serpent to tempt her to join in his rebellion against God. Though on the surface the temptation was simply to disobey God by eating a forbidden fruit, the temptation went much deeper: to doubt God's love, word, and care. When both Adam and Eve disobeyed God, trying to be like Him in knowing both good and evil, they fractured His perfect creation. They realized their nakedness and were ashamed. Their act of open rebellion against God now infects all things, and through their sin pain, decay, and death came to all creation. Their lives and the lives of their future offspring would be infected by the inescapable pattern of sin and death.

Yet, in all this, God chose not to abandon Adam, Eve, and all of His creation. Instead, God confronted Adam, Eve, and Satan in the now corrupted paradise, and He made promises. Because of their disobedience and doubt of God's command, Adam and Eve would die, and their lives would constantly be a struggle for survival.

Even so, God promised that one day an offspring of Eve would crush Satan, undoing and reversing the damage that Satan, sin, and death had brought into the world. God promised to salvage and restore humanity and creation despite mankind's continual rebellion. Adam and Eve, and their offspring, would have to wait and cling to God's promise of restoration. The rest of the narratives of Scripture, as well as all human history, hinged on this promise. In Jesus Christ, the promise was fulfilled when He died on the cross to pay the penalty for mankind's rebellion and made us right with God. Through Jesus, the death that entered the world through the rebellion of Adam and Eve is overcome, and we will be with Him in the new creation one day.

REFLECTION: How does Jesus' victory over sin and death change how you live each day? How can thanking God daily for your forgiveness impact how you interact with people in the world as you await Jesus' return and the restoration of paradise?

DAY 4: CAIN AND ABEL

> The LORD said to Cain, "Why are you angry, and why has your face fallen? If you do well, will you not be accepted? And if you do not do well, sin is crouching at the door. Its desire is contrary to you, but you must rule over it." (GENESIS 4:6–7)

After their rebellion, Adam and Eve were forced out of the Garden of Eden to farm the land. Though they could not eat of the tree of life, God did not abandon them. Adam and Eve worked the ground, and Eve bore children.

The first son mentioned was named Cain and the second Abel. Cain worked the ground and Abel tended sheep. In this apparently thriving society of the first family, with it being likely that generations were gathered, Cain and Abel both offered sacrifices of their labors to God. We learn from the Book of Hebrews (11:4) that Abel offered his sacrifice in faith while Cain did not, so God favored Abel's sacrifice. With this, the corruption of sin that had begun in Cain's parents now festered in him, and he became wrathful toward his younger brother. God even confronted Cain, warning him to master his sinful anger before it led to temptation and evil, but Cain dismissed God's warnings.

Cain then lured his brother out into a field and murdered him. The sin of the parents was now manifested in their son. Again, God confronted Cain, calling him to repent, but Cain, like his parents, tried to cover his wrongdoing. Whereas God had every right to destroy Cain, He instead showed him mercy by marking him so that other descendants of Adam and Eve would not avenge Abel. Cain's life was a testimony to the reality that judgment belongs to God and not to man.

God's offer of forgiveness through the coming Savior was there for him, but Cain turned his back on God and left the family to start his own clan. So God provided a new heir to Adam and Eve named Seth, who acted as a new firstborn son to carry the line of the promised Messiah into the future. Just as He had done with Adam and Eve, God showed a commitment to care for and restore His creation, preserving His chosen people and the family line for the sake of His promises that would come to pass in the Savior, Jesus Christ.

REFLECTION: What are some ways you have given in to the temptations of your sinful flesh and abandoned the responsibilities God has given you in life? How has God remained faithful to you in your life even when you have failed to remain faithful to Him?

DAY 5: NOAH AND THE FLOOD

> And God said, "This is the sign of the covenant that I make between Me and you and every living creature that is with you, for all future generations: I have set My bow in the cloud, and it shall be a sign of the covenant between Me and the earth." (GENESIS 9:12–13)

As the generations came and went after Cain and Abel, more and more of Adam and Eve's offspring followed Cain's path. Self-centered violence and exploitation escalated throughout the earth without any checks. As the number of faithful believers from Seth's line dwindled, God was deeply hurt and regretted ever creating humans. He decided to send a flood to purge the earth of sinful humanity.

But God had mercy on one man from the line of Seth named Noah. By God's grace, Noah still clung to God's promise of the Savior, so God instructed him to save a remnant of humanity and the land animals and birds by building a giant ship—an ark. In a global flood, God destroyed all other humans and animals, then replenished the earth's populations through the survivors in the ark. God then promised to preserve His creation by not sending another flood, and He set His bow in the sky as a sign of His relenting from this sort of cataclysm ever again.

Unfortunately, Noah and his wife watched the same pattern resume that Adam and Eve once saw—as more and more of their offspring wandered from the faith. Generation by generation, the number of those who clung to God and His promises dwindled again. Once more, God would have to step in to human history to keep His promise of salvation through Christ intact.

Throughout this first section of the Bible account in the Book of Genesis, we see this similar pattern: God creates, people rebel, judgment comes, yet God stays faithful to His promises. This central theme continues throughout the Bible and, if we are honest with ourselves, into our own lives. Though we continually sin and act as if we know better than God, He is faithful and just to forgive our sins and cleanse us from unrighteousness in Christ. Thanks be to God!

REFLECTION: What is something you can do in your own life to remind yourself to daily pray, confessing your sins to God and thanking Him for forgiveness in Christ? Consider picking a time, place, or other routine for prayers of confession and thanks that works in your daily life.

God's Plan for Abraham

DAY 1: GOD CALLS ABRAM

> Now the LORD said to Abram, "Go from your country and your kindred and your father's house to the land that I will show you. And I will make of you a great nation, and I will bless you and make your name great, so that you will be a blessing. I will bless those who bless you, and him who dishonors you I will curse, and in you all the families of the earth shall be blessed." (GENESIS 12:1–3)

God had saved Noah and his family from the flood for the sake of His promise to send the Savior. Even so, because of the corruption of sin passed down from generation to generation, Noah's descendants grew more wicked. They rejected God's purpose for their lives and His promised salvation. Instead of abandoning creation, however, God chose a third husband and wife, Abram and Sarai. Through them, God would raise up a new nation through which His blessings would flow out to all mankind—particularly the Savior promised to Adam and Eve.

God called Abram to leave his fatherland in Mesopotamia and travel with his wife, Sarai, to a land God would reveal along the way. God made four great promises to Abram: to make Abram the father of a great nation; to make Abram's name (reputation) great; to bless those who bless Abram and curse those who curse him; and to bless all the families of the earth through Abram.

In choosing Abram and Sarai, God did not abandon all other nations. Instead, He was creating this new nation by grace. In it He would concentrate His revelations concerning the life and work of the coming Savior who would be born in this nation. He set this new nation in the midst of the unbelieving nations so that all people could learn the mighty acts of Abram's God and learn of the Messiah from the revelations given to Abram's offspring.

REFLECTION: How does Christ's Church today work in a similar way to God's chosen family and nation in Abram's time? How does this comparison give us comfort as we live out the Christian life in our congregations and households today?

DAY 2: GOD TESTS ABRAHAM

So Abraham called the name of that place, "The Lord will provide"; as it is said to this day, "On the mount of the Lord it shall be provided." (Genesis 22:14)

After being chosen by God, Abram and Sarai obeyed God and traveled to Canaan, the land God promised to give their descendants. Abram built altars to give thanks to God for His promise. Already the nations were being blessed through Abram and the promise of his great descendant, the Savior. Yet with all these promises being fulfilled, the couple still waited. Twenty-four years passed, and Sarai remained childless.

Then when Abram was ninety-nine and Sarai eighty-nine, God appeared to Abram and changed his name to Abraham and Sarai's to Sarah. God promised that by the same time next year Sarah would have the promised child. Though Sarah laughed at the preposterousness of this at her age, God kept His word. Isaac, Abraham's beloved son, was born.

Some years later, God tested Abraham, commanding him to burn his beloved, only son Isaac as a human sacrifice on a mountain God would show him. At the last moment, an angel commanded Abraham not to harm his son. God provided a substitute sacrifice, a ram caught in the thicket by its horns. Abraham sacrificed the ram in place of his son Isaac.

This is a clear picture of the saving work of the promised Savior. Like the ram, Christ's head would be encircled with thorns and God's only beloved Son sacrificed in the place of all sinners. The picture of the Savior's saving sacrifice was becoming clearer. He would crush the serpent's head by removing the curse of sin from us and taking that curse upon Himself. And on this same mountain, about a thousand years later, Solomon would build God's temple. On the same mountain, a thousand years after that, God the Father would sacrifice His only begotten Son, crowned with thorns, to save us from our sins. God's plan of salvation, first mentioned in the fall, is building more and more of its epic shape.

REFLECTION: In your own life, when does God feel the furthest away or most distant? Why? How can Christ's promise that He is with you always offer comfort in those times?

DAY 3: JACOB STEALS ISAAC'S BLESSING

[God said to Jacob,] "Behold, I am with you and will keep you wherever you go, and will bring you back to this land. For I will not leave you until I have done what I have promised you." (GENESIS 28:15)

When Isaac grew up, his mother, Sarah, died. Abraham got a wife for him from his relatives in Mesopotamia, and her name was Rebekah. God gave Rebekah twin sons and told her those sons would grow into two great nations; the younger would be greater than the older. God extended the promise He had given Abraham to Isaac—that all people would be blessed through his offspring, the coming Savior (Genesis 26:1–5).

The twins were named Esau and Jacob. They were exact opposites—Esau was an outdoorsman and a hunter, hairy, and flighty. Jacob was quieter, preferring to stay around the tents with his mother. Though Isaac knew God had chosen Jacob and rejected Esau, Esau was still his favorite. Both twins were very worldly, giving little if any thought to God and His glorious promise. Though Esau as firstborn had the right of the double inheritance, including the line that would lead to the Messiah, he sold it to Jacob for a bowl of stew.

Later, Rebekah and Jacob tricked the aged Isaac into giving Jacob the blessing he wanted to give Esau. With Esau angry enough to murder him, Jacob fled for his life. Along the way, God appeared to him in a dream, passing to him the promise He had given Abraham and Isaac to bless all nations through his offspring—the promised Savior. Though this blessed family was continually broken by the persistence of sin, God was faithful to His promises and took care of them.

REFLECTION: How has sin broken or stained family relationships in your life? Knowing that God in Christ has reconciled you to Himself, what can you do to help reconcile a broken relationship in your family?

DAY 4: JACOB'S TWELVE SONS

So Jacob called the name of the place Peniel, saying, "For I have seen God face to face, and yet my life has been delivered." (GENESIS 32:30)

After receiving his vision from God, Jacob travelled to Mesopotamia. He lived with his mother Rebekah's brother, Laban, and became a shepherd of Laban's flocks. Because of God's blessing passed on to him from Isaac, Jacob was blessed, and the flocks under his care grew mightily, which made Laban wealthy. Wanting to keep Jacob with him, Laban offered the hand of his beautiful daughter Rachel, whom Jacob loved, in marriage. But on the wedding night, Laban deceived Jacob and gave him Leah, Rachel's not nearly as attractive older sister. Then Laban promised to give Jacob Rachel as his second wife as well if Jacob would serve him another seven years. Jacob, who had previously deceived his father, was now deceived by his uncle.

When God saw how Jacob loved his wife Rachel and resented his wife Leah, He opened Leah's womb and gave her four sons and a daughter. Leah's fourth son, Judah, would continue the line leading to the promised Savior. Leah wanted her husband's love, but an intense hostility and competition grew between the two sisters instead.

Rachel remained childless and gave her maid to Jacob as a minor wife to give him a form of surrogate son, and she bore Jacob two sons. In retaliation, Leah did the same with her own maid, giving Jacob two more sons, and Leah conceived and gave Jacob two more sons of her own. Finally, God answered Rachel's prayer, and she gave birth to Joseph, Jacob's eleventh son. Later, Rachel gave birth to Jacob's twelfth son as Jacob returned to Canaan, but she died in childbirth. These twelve sons would be the fathers of the twelve tribes of God's chosen nation.

Jacob lived with Laban a total of twenty years, raising great herds and flocks for himself despite the fact that Laban kept trying to cheat him out of his wages. After this time, God told Jacob to return home. Jacob feared meeting his brother, Esau, whom he understandably expected to be harboring a murderous grudge. The night before their meeting, however, Jacob wrestled with a stranger who turned out to be God Himself. The Lord changed Jacob's name to Israel—which means "he who struggles with God." This would be the name of the nation God had promised to Abraham, Isaac, and Jacob. When Israel met Esau the next morning, Esau received him joyfully. Despite the layered brokenness of the family, God provided them with the power to reconcile—just as He has power to reconcile sinful mankind to Himself through the Savior.

REFLECTION: Consider a time when you may have had doubts about your faith, but in the end God's Word prevailed and strengthened your faith instead. What did this struggle show you about God's faithfulness? How did it work to form your faith?

DAY 5: JOSEPH SOLD AS A SLAVE

> But Joseph said to them, "Do not fear, for am I in the place of God? As for you, you meant evil against me, but God meant it for good, to bring it about that many people should be kept alive, as they are today." (GENESIS 50:19–20)

Back in Canaan, the brokenness of Jacob's (now renamed Israel) family continued to divide and consume them. Israel loved Joseph far more than all his other sons because Joseph was born of his beloved wife Rachel. Israel treated him far better than his brothers, even giving him a special robe. Joseph boasted of dreams God had given of a future glory he would have.

When shepherding the flocks far away from home, the older brothers saw their despised brother Joseph coming over the hills toward them, wearing the expensive robe Jacob had given him. They plotted to kill him but sold him to merchants headed toward Egypt instead, lying to their father by saying Joseph was killed by wild animals.

Then as a slave in Egypt, Joseph was sold to an Egyptian official. God was with him even in captivity. Joseph served loyally and faithfully and was promoted to take charge of everything in his master's house and business. However, his master's wife tried to seduce him, and when Joseph refused, she accused him of attempted rape. Joseph was imprisoned.

But even in the prison, Joseph was blessed by God, and he was given charge over the prisoners in his section. Two years later, Pharaoh, king of Egypt, had dreams about cattle and sheaves consuming one another that no one in Egypt could interpret. One of Joseph's former prison mates, for whom Joseph had once interpreted a dream, remembered Joseph, who was then brought to Pharaoh and interpreted his dreams. The dreams foretold seven years of plentiful harvests followed by seven years of complete famine.

Joseph advised Pharaoh to store up grain in the upcoming good years to feed the people during the famine. Pharaoh appointed Joseph to store up the food and lead as his right-hand man. Joseph provided not only for Egypt but also for many neighboring nations and his own family. Joseph's brothers came to Egypt seeking food, and after testing them and finding their repentance sincere, he revealed himself to them and brought his father's family to live in Egypt, where they multiplied into a great nation.

Here is another clear revelation of the promised Christ. Like Joseph, He would be rejected by His own brothers and taken in chains to another leader—the Roman governor. But through His sufferings, Jesus would save all people from their sins, then rise on the third day, and ascend to the Father's right hand in heaven, where He governs all things that happen in creation for the good of His Church.

REFLECTION: What is one role you have in life where God has called you to take care of people? Pray that God would strengthen you today to live out that role faithfully and joyfully, and so be God's hands and feet in caring for His creation through you.

The Passover Lamb

DAY 1: GOD CALLS MOSES

> God said to Moses, "I AM WHO I AM." And He said, "Say this to the people of Israel: 'I AM has sent me to you.'" (EXODUS 3:14)

Through God's faithfulness to His promises, Joseph brought his father Jacob's family to Egypt to provide for them during the seven years of famine. After Joseph and his brothers died, their descendants remained in Egypt and multiplied into a great nation. However, the Egyptians feared and enslaved them for the next four hundred years. God's people cried out to Him, and He heard their cries for help. He raised up a deliverer for them named Moses.

Moses was born at a time when the Pharaoh commanded the Hebrews' male babies to be thrown into the Nile River. Instead of killing him, Moses' mother placed him in a basket of reeds in the Nile River. Pharaoh's daughter found the basket, had compassion on the boy, and adopted Moses as her own son, raising him as an adopted prince of Egypt in Pharaoh's own house.

When Moses was forty, however, he killed an Egyptian to defend the Hebrew slave the Egyptian was beating. When the news spread, Moses fled for his life to live as an exile in the land of Midian, fearing the wrath of Pharaoh. Starting a brand-new life, Moses married a Midianite woman and became a shepherd of his father-in-law's flocks under Mount Sinai. Forty years later at the age of eighty, while shepherding the flocks, Moses saw a bush burning on Mount Sinai. Though burning, the bush was not consumed by the fire. Going to investigate, Moses heard God call from the burning bush commanding him to return to Egypt and to order Pharaoh to release the Hebrews. Moses was reluctant but eventually went to do God's work. God would remain faithful to His promises to Abraham and his descendants to bring them to the Promised Land, where one day the Savior of the world would be born.

REFLECTION: What are some life experiences that, at the time, did not seem important but now have proved useful in your daily life of faith? How can you use those experiences to better love and serve your neighbor in the name of Christ?

DAY 2: THE PASSOVER

> [God said,] "For I will pass through the land of Egypt that night, and I will strike all the firstborn in the land of Egypt, both man and beast; and on all the gods of Egypt I will execute judgments: I am the LORD." (EXODUS 12:12)

Moses went back to Egypt, the land of his youth, and told Pharaoh, the powerful king of the ancient empire of Egypt, God's command to release the Hebrews. Pharaoh hardened his heart and refused to obey, instead punishing the Hebrew slaves in Egypt. In response, God sent a series of increasingly devastating plagues to bring Pharaoh to repentance and obedience. The plagues also served to demonstrate to the world for all time God's authority and supreme power over all things. Despite these plagues, Pharaoh continued to refuse, until the tenth plague in which all firstborn males were put to death in Egypt.

To protect His people from the angel of death during this tenth plague, God commanded His people, slaves in Egypt, to slaughter a lamb and spread its blood over the doorways of their houses. The angel of death saw the blood and passed over the house, sparing the firstborn. This Passover was the plague which freed Israel, and the annual festival of remembrance became the most important festival in Israel's religious year. This Passover event was the third really clear picture in Scripture of the sacrifice of the coming Savior, the first being the promise of crushing the serpent's head and the second being the ram caught in the thorns that was sacrificed in place of Isaac. Christ is the true and ultimate Passover Lamb, whose blood shed on the cross marks us by faith and saves us from eternal punishment on Judgment Day.

Pharaoh compelled the Israelites to leave Egypt, then changed his mind when they were camped by the Red Sea. He commanded his army to recapture them, and when the Israelites saw the Egyptian chariots and horses, they cried out in fear. In response, God, through Moses, divided the Red Sea with a mighty wind, and Israel passed through on dry ground. When the Egyptian army pursued them, God closed the Red Sea over the Egyptians and destroyed them. God had worked His salvation by not only delivering His people from slavery but by destroying their enemies as well.

REFLECTION: How do the events of the Passover and the exodus relate to what God has done for the Church today in Jesus? How does this impact how you view the world and your place in it?

DAY 3: MOUNT SINAI

> [Moses said,] "The LORD your God will raise up for you a prophet like me from among you, from your brothers—it is to Him you shall listen."
> (DEUTERONOMY 18:15)

Before bringing the Hebrews into the Promised Land of Canaan, God led them to Mount Sinai. This was the same place in the wilderness where God had appeared to Moses in the burning bush. This time, however, God came down to meet the whole nation. Not only the bush but the entire mountain was burning with God's presence! He spoke the words of the Ten Commandments to the people that they might fear, love, and trust in Him above all gods of the nations around them and to know how to love their neighbors as themselves.

The people were terrified by God's presence and thundering voice, so they begged for Moses to go up the mountain to listen to God so that he could relay God's message to them. Despite their many failures to follow Him, God remained faithful to His promise, and the people promised to obey God's commands.

Moses spent forty days on Mount Sinai receiving the Ten Commandments on two stone tablets, along with a design for a portable worship space called the tent of meeting or tabernacle. In that tabernacle, God would dwell among His people, and there they could approach Him, confessing their sins, making sacrifices, and receiving His forgiveness. On Mount Sinai, Moses received the contents of the Book of Leviticus, which lays out the rules governing worship, festivals, and the sacrifices, which all pointed ahead to the coming sacrifice of God's ultimate and final Passover Lamb, the promised Christ.

Moses led Israel from Mount Sinai to the southern border of the Promised Land, but they refused to trust God and go in to battle the mightier Canaanite nations. For their unbelief, they were sentenced to wander in the wilderness forty years until that generation died and their children grew to take their place. Moses led them all through the forty years and died right before it was time for the next generation to go over into the Promised Land.

Shortly before he died, Moses preached a series of farewell sermons that make up the Book of Deuteronomy. In them, he prophesied the coming Christ, saying, "The LORD your God will raise up for you a prophet like me from among you, from your brothers—it is to Him you shall listen" (Deuteronomy 18:15). Jesus Christ is that prophet like Moses. God's mighty Son came in humility as our human brother, a child of Adam and Eve like us, that we might hear God's word of grace and mercy and find salvation in Him alone.

REFLECTION: Consider the importance in your own life of law and order, rules and regulations. Pray that God would strengthen you as His redeemed child in Christ to eagerly and joyfully seek to follow God's commands in your life today.

DAY 4: JOSHUA AND THE JUDGES

[God said to Joshua,] "Have I not commanded you? Be strong and coura-geous. Do not be frightened, and do not be dismayed, for the LORD your God is with you wherever you go." (JOSHUA 1:9)

After Moses died, God raised up his assistant and aide Joshua to lead Israel into the Promised Land. Under Joshua's leadership, God conquered the Canaanite nations and gave the land to Abraham's descendants as He had promised. In a sense, Joshua was a forerunner of Jesus, who conquered all our enemies through His death on the cross and leads us into the promised land of the new heavens and the new earth when He returns in glory. In fact, the names *Joshua* and *Jesus* have nearly identical meanings but in different languages.

Upon Joshua's death, the twelve tribes of Israel held and occupied the core, but not all, of the Promised Land, and the might of the Canaanite nations was broken. As the twelve tribes grew stronger and more numerous in coming generations, God instructed them to drive out the remaining Canaanites from their border and possess all the land God intended for them. If they did this, then they would be insulated from the false religious practices and influences of their neighbors, be able to worship God in the purity of the worship God had given on Mount Sinai through Moses, and be witnesses to the nations around them and those that passed through their trade routes. But the Israelites failed to obey God, and the false idolatry of the Canaanites persisted in and around the Promised Land.

The Israelites grew curious about how their neighboring nations worshiped their gods. Periodically and consistently, they turned away to worship these false gods and idols. To preserve His people and restore them, God brought in neighboring nations who conquered Israel and made their lives miserable. Just like they had in Egypt, the Israelites called out to God, and He had mercy and raised up tribal chieftains called judges to deliver them and govern them. The people remained faithful for the most part during the life of their judges, but once the judge died, they drifted away from the Lord again. The sad, ever-plunging cycle is recorded in the Book of Judges.

REFLECTION: Looking at your life, what is something that consistently tempts you away from following God's will faithfully? What can you, as God's redeemed child in Christ, do to remove or mitigate that temptation from your life so you can more joyfully go about your life of faith?

DAY 5: KING SAUL

> Whenever the LORD raised up judges for them, the LORD was with the judge, and He saved them from the hand of their enemies all the days of the judge. For the LORD was moved to pity by their groaning because of those who afflicted and oppressed them. (JUDGES 2:18)

The time of the judges grew worse and worse for the people of Israel as "everyone did what was right in his own eyes" (Judges 21:25). God's people falsely concluded the endless cycle of invasions was because they did not have a strong central ruler like every other nation, not because they had turned their backs on God. They demanded a king.

God raised one final judge for them named Samuel. Samuel was unique among the judges. He was not only a ruler but also a great prophet and a priest. He likewise gave us a glimpse of the coming Savior, who will serve as King over all God's people, the great Prophet who brings us God's Word, and the great High Priest who offers Himself to satisfy God's wrath at our sins and win our forgiveness.

Rejecting God as their King and refusing to follow His noble Law, the Israelites demanded an earthly king. In response, God directed Samuel to anoint the man the Lord chose. God chose a humble yet physically imposing man from the smallest tribe in Israel, the tribe descended from Jacob's twelfth son, Benjamin. The man's name was Saul.

Samuel anointed Saul as king, and he was filled with the Holy Spirit, equipped for his mission as Israel's king. Saul was able to work side by side with the chief priests who had charge of the worship in Israel and teaching about God. At first, Saul did well, delivering Israel from its enemies. But later he grew proud, and instead of carefully following God's commands, he did what was right in his own eyes. God rejected him for his disobedience and removed the Holy Spirit from him. Saul grew fearful, suspicious, and insecure in his rule. God could have, and in many respects should have, left Israel to suffer the consequences it deserved. Instead, He had mercy and chose a man after His own heart to replace Saul as king of Israel. God remained faithful to His promise and remained with His people.

REFLECTION: Consider a time when you thought you knew better than God or what God's Word says, and it turned out disastrous for you. Then, thank God that He has remained faithful to you through Christ despite your failings.

Slaying the Giant

DAY 1: THE PROMISE OF THE SON OF DAVID

> [God said to David,] "And your house and your kingdom shall be made sure forever before Me. Your throne shall be established forever." (2 SAMUEL 7:16)

After King Saul disobeyed God, the Lord rejected him as king of Israel and withdrew His Holy Spirit from him. Saul became just a shell of the man he was early in his reign when the Spirit had worked so mightily within him.

God then secretly sent Samuel to the city of Bethlehem in the tribe of Judah to anoint David king over Israel. David, the youngest son of a large family, was a man after God's own heart. At his anointing, the Holy Spirit rushed upon David, and his victory over Goliath the giant showed how bold the Spirit made him. In the king's service, David was extremely loyal to Saul, and David's courage and strength in the Spirit enabled him to lead the army of Israel to great victories.

Those great victories and the praises raised toward David should have made Saul thankful—instead, he was overcome with jealousy. That jealousy turned to murderous suspicion, and Saul even made open attempts on David's life. Finally, David had to flee and go into hiding while Saul pursued him with Israel's army. Twice David had the opportunity to assassinate Saul, but he refused to raise his hand against the Lord's anointed, choosing instead to commend himself into God's hand and let God deal with Saul. Eventually, Saul was wounded in battle and in his despair took his own life.

David became king, and in his reign, David defeated all of Israel's enemies and won peace on every side. He expanded Israel's borders to where God had intended back in the days of Joshua, and he captured Jerusalem, making it his capital. David brought the ark of the covenant into the city.

After this, David wanted to build a magnificent temple in Jerusalem. The Lord, however, forbade him because of all the war, violence, and blood David had shed in defense of God's people. War, punishment, and death all fall under the Law. God instead wanted His temple built in a reign of peace—the reign of David's son Solomon. But God promised David He would build a house for him, that is, one of David's descendants would be the promised Savior who would reign eternally. That is why Jesus is often called the Son of David in the Gospels.

David stored up vast quantities of construction supplies for the temple and organized the Levites, the tribe from which Moses came, to lead the worship at the future temple and to guard the holy things as the Law of Moses required.

REFLECTION: What makes a relationship of a king to his subjects different from other leaders to people under their authority? Why is it so important for us to think of Jesus as our King?

DAY 2: SOLOMON BUILDS THE TEMPLE, STRAYS FROM GOD

The fear of the LORD is the beginning of knowledge; fools despise wisdom and instruction. (PROVERBS 1:7)

D avid was not a perfect king, but for the most part he set his heart on serving God and the people of God entrusted to him. He was succeeded by his young son Solomon, who after coming to power made a great sacrifice to the Lord at the tabernacle at Gibeon. There, God appeared to him in a dream and told him to ask for whatever he wanted. Instead of asking for wealth or power, Solomon asked for discretion to know how to lead God's great people. This pleased the Lord greatly because Solomon was seeking this wisdom for the benefit of God's people—the way his father, David, had ruled Israel.

God gave Solomon discretion as well as great wisdom, which in turn brought great wealth and prestige. Solomon built the temple his father, David, had prepared. He built it on Mount Moriah, the same place God had provided a sacrifice for Abraham. It is near this very spot where one day Jesus, the Son of David and the final sacrifice, would suffer the wrath of God on a cross to bring forgiveness and eternal life to God's people. The temple symbolized God's permanent presence among His people. The transition from the portable tabernacle to the permanent temple also represented Christ dwelling among His scattered Church until Judgment Day, when He will return visibly to dwell with us permanently in the new heavens and the new earth.

Solomon, however, broke several of God's laws later in his illustrious reign. In particular, he broke Moses' command forbidding a king to marry women from other nations. Solomon married these foreign women to establish peace with their nations, but these women led him astray to idolatry. He built temples to the false gods of foreign nations in Israel and even worshiped the gods.

In response, God told Solomon He would take the kingdom from Solomon's son. For David's sake, and God's promise of the Savior King, God would permit Solomon's descendants to reign over the tribe of Judah as kings. Ten of the other tribes would be ruled by another Israelite king. After Solomon died, ten northern tribes split off and formed their own kingdom called Israel. David's descendants ruled the Southern Kingdom called Judah. The unfaithfulness of Solomon manifested itself in the twin countries of God's people and the tension that always existed between them.

REFLECTION: Consider something in your own life that at first seemed good and helpful but has since introduced harm to your spiritual life. What is it, and what can you do to remove that from your life so that you can instead focus on your identity as a baptized child of God?

DAY 3: THE RISE AND FALL OF THE NORTHERN KINGDOM

When Ahab saw Elijah, Ahab said to him, "Is it you, you troubler of Israel?" And he answered, "I have not troubled Israel, but you have, and your father's house, because you have abandoned the commandments of the LORD and followed the Baals." (1 KINGS 18:17–18)

When Solomon's son Rehoboam became king, he refused to lighten the heavy tax load Solomon had imposed. This created great strife and unrest among God's people. Ten tribes to the north of Judah rebelled, broke off, and formed their own kingdom called Israel.

Their first king, Jeroboam, feared his subjects would return to the king of Judah if they went to the temple for the required feasts. So he built two temples of his own in the north and south ends of his kingdom, promoting a false religion in the kingdom of Israel. Sadly, none of the kings of Israel after him ever repented of that sin by destroying the false temples.

Israel was then ruled by a series of dynasties. All the kings of all the dynasties were wicked, with some worse than others. Overall, Israel was prosperous—financially and numerically—and militarily strong. But the kingdom was very disobedient to the Lord. When idolatry and wickedness was at its worst in Israel under King Ahab and his wicked queen, Jezebel, God sent two of the greatest early prophets: Elijah and Elisha.

The first of these men, Elijah, was a fiery prophet who called Israel to repent and return to the Lord. When Ahab refused, Elijah declared a drought that lasted three-and-a-half years. At the end of this time, Elijah held a famous contest against the prophets of the false god Baal. Baal's prophets slayed a bull for an offering and spent all day calling on Baal to set it aflame—but nothing happened. Then late in the afternoon, Elijah slayed a bull, laid it on a heap of wood, and drenched it in water. He prayed, and immediately fire came down from heaven and consumed the bull, the wood, the water, and even the dirt and rocks. God demonstrated that He alone was the true God in all Israel.

Elisha was a partner to Elijah and succeeded him when Elijah was taken up alive into heaven. Both Elijah and Elisha raised dead children. Elisha also cleansed a leper, and God worked other miracles through him. But despite these great prophets, the leaders and people of Israel continued worshiping Baal and other false gods. Ultimately, God brought in the mighty Assyrian army to capture and exile the nation. The nation disappeared and became known as the Ten Lost Tribes.

REFLECTION: What role does disciplining children play in the life of a parent? How does that relate to God's interaction with His people in the Old Testament? Pray a prayer of thanks to God for sending His Son, Jesus, our Brother, who lived perfect obedience in our place.

DAY 4: FAITHFUL KINGS, JUDAH'S SIN AND ITS FALL

The LORD, the God of their fathers, sent persistently to them by His messengers, because He had compassion on His people and on His dwelling place. But they kept mocking the messengers of God, despising His words and scoffing at His prophets, until the wrath of the LORD rose against His people, until there was no remedy. (2 CHRONICLES 36:15–16)

When God's people split into two kingdoms, David's descendants continued to rule in the south. This small kingdom was made up of two tribes—Judah and Benjamin. The kings of Judah were a mix of good and evil kings, but among the good kings two were notable in comparison to David in terms of their wholehearted devotion to the Lord: Hezekiah and Josiah.

Hezekiah was king in Judah at the time when God brought in the Assyrian Empire to crush the Northern Kingdom of Israel. The Assyrians, to that point the greatest empire in the world, continued their conquest and swept to the south, surrounding Jerusalem. On the verge of seeming annihilation of his kingdom, King Hezekiah heard God's words of comfort through the prophet Isaiah, and that night, God's angel killed 185,000 soldiers of the besieging Assyrian army, and the kingdom of Judah was saved.

Josiah, one of the last kings in Judah, was restoring the badly neglected temple when the workers discovered an important scroll of Scripture that had apparently been hidden in a treasury box in the temple. The scroll threatened destruction and exile for Israel's idolatry. Josiah, with his prophet Jeremiah, called Judah to repentance, tearing down the idols and high places that had been lingering in Judah, some since the time of the conquest of the Promised Land. Though Josiah worked great reform, the damage was already done, and God's people persisted in their unfaithfulness.

Overall, Judah lasted longer than Israel, but because of its increasing wickedness and idolatry, it was conquered by Babylon and many of its people taken away into exile. The people of Judah had a foolish expectation that the temple was like a good luck charm and God would protect the temple and Jerusalem no matter how wicked the people became. In the end, God permitted the temple to be looted and burned to the ground. Now, both the Northern and Southern Kingdoms were conquered and scattered, yet God remained faithful to His promises to His people even in these darkest times.

REFLECTION: What are ways that Christians today find their confidence, identity, security, and meaning in things that are not Christ? What is one habit you can form to help keep your focus squarely on the Savior of the world, Jesus Christ?

DAY 5: THE TEMPLE IS DESTROYED, GOD RAISES UP DANIEL

> Behold, the days are coming, declares the LORD, when I will fulfill the promise I made to the house of Israel and the house of Judah. In those days and at that time I will cause a righteous Branch to spring up for David, and He shall execute justice and righteousness in the land. In those days Judah will be saved, and Jerusalem will dwell securely. And this is the name by which it will be called: "The LORD is our righteousness." (JEREMIAH 33:14–16)

The defeat of Judah was complicated. The Babylonians actually conquered Jerusalem twice. The first time, they exiled the king, the nobles, and every skilled craftsman, leaving the poorest of the poor behind with a puppet king they thought would pay their tribute and be loyal. At that time, they kept the temple and city intact.

Previously, God had raised up the great prophet Jeremiah, who warned Judah to repent or the Babylonians would conquer it. After the first conquest, he remained behind with the poor to guide them so they would repent and restore correct worship at the temple. Unfortunately, the people grew even more wicked and proud—thinking they were the chosen because the exile of the others meant they could live in the grander homes now left vacant.

Among the exiles from this first conquest that were now scattered throughout the Babylonian Empire, there was optimism that their exile would be short because the temple was still standing. For those exiles, God raised up one of their priests, Ezekiel, to be a prophet. He warned the people that because of the unrepentance of the priests and those remaining in Jerusalem, the city would be conquered once more and the temple would be destroyed.

When Judah's final puppet king broke his sworn promise to the Babylonian emperor and turned to the Egyptians for aid, God brought the Babylonian army back to lay siege to Jerusalem. When it fell, the temple was destroyed, the city walls broken down, the king blinded and led off in chains, and all but the poorest of the poor exiled.

It looked very bleak for the exiles. Like the ten tribes of the north, it seemed likely they would disappear from history as well. But God had a promise to keep to David, so He raised up a young man named Daniel and prepared him for government service in Babylon to help ensure the survival of Judah until it was time to return to Jerusalem and rebuild the temple in preparation for the coming of the Christ.

Throughout everything, God remained with His people, even in the darkest times.

REFLECTION: Consider what factors in your life led you to the greatest amount of depression and despair, and why. Remember that God is with you no matter the circumstances and still speaks to you, His redeemed child, through His Word. Identify some Bible verses that convey God's care and power in your life, and work on either memorizing those or placing them in locations of importance where you can refer to them often.

Delivered from the Lions

> I make a decree, that in all my royal dominion people are to tremble and fear before the God of Daniel, for He is the living God, enduring forever; His kingdom shall never be destroyed, and His dominion shall be to the end. He delivers and rescues; He works signs and wonders in heaven and on earth, He who has saved Daniel from the power of the lions. (DANIEL 6:26–27)

Judah could have disappeared in the grave of the Babylonian exile, but God instead raised up prophets and leaders to preserve it through its roughly seventy years of exile. Daniel became a powerful prophet and influential government official in Babylon during those years. When Babylon was overthrown by the Persians, Daniel was promoted to a high position in the Persian Empire, stirring the jealousy-based charges that led him to the lions' den. Daniel's enemies created a plot whereby they trapped the king into executing Daniel for his religious beliefs by throwing him into a den of lions. God saved Daniel, and when Daniel survived, no doubt the fear of Daniel and his God won greater favor and protection for the exiled Jews.

Around the same time, a new day for God's people dawned when the new Persian emperor announced his edict permitting the Jews to return to rebuild the temple in Jerusalem. The Jews returned from their exile—but that did not mean everything was easy for them. Great opposition arose against them from neighbors, including the Samaritans. Even when the temple was rebuilt and worship finally restored, great peril rose against the people of God. Later, God raised up Esther, a Jewish woman who became the queen of a Persian emperor. Her intervention saved the Jews from another threat to their very existence.

With the temple rebuilt and the people protected, things were nearly ready for the Messiah to be born. It would still be hundreds of years of error from within and enemies from without, but God's people were back in the Promised Land awaiting the coming of the promised Savior.

REFLECTION: Consider a position or role in your life where God has given you the opportunity to love and serve your neighbor. Who are those neighbors, and how can you follow the example of people like Daniel and Esther to faithfully love and serve them today?

DAY 2: THE TIME BETWEEN THE TESTAMENTS

Behold, I will send you Elijah the prophet before the great and awesome day of the LORD comes. And he will turn the hearts of fathers to their children and the hearts of children to their fathers, lest I come and strike the land with a decree of utter destruction. (MALACHI 4:5–6)

The Old Testament came to a close less than a hundred years after the rebuilding of the temple. In the final book of the Old Testament, the prophet Malachi called upon the priests and people to clean up their sacrificial practices. He also called upon them to stop neglecting to support the Levites, the tribe of Israel that was essential for the proper functioning of the temple and the ongoing instruction of the people. He also announced the coming Savior who would suddenly come to this new temple and the prophet like Elijah who would precede Him. The Savior is Jesus and the prophet John the Baptist.

Four hundred years stretched between the close of the Old Testament and the birth of Christ, but they were very eventful years on the world stage. The Persian Empire was destroyed by Alexander the Great, and he spread the Greek culture throughout the Mediterranean world, including Judah.

After Alexander's death, his four generals divided up his territory and were in constant competition and conflict with one another. The Jews found themselves in the middle of these conflicts. For a very short period, they broke free and even obtained a level of autonomy. Then the Roman Empire grew, Judah became a vassal state, and it was finally annexed by the Romans.

After Julius Caesar was assassinated, a civil war developed between Roman leaders named Octavius and Marc Antony. A young ruler named Herod gave his support to Octavius. When Octavius became the second emperor of Rome, he gave Herod the title King Herod and extensive land including Jerusalem and Judea to rule. The Roman Senate gave Octavius the title Caesar Augustus. The political stage was now set for the coming of the Christ.

REFLECTION: What are some of the major political and historical forces that have shaped your life? How has God remained faithful to you during this time? What does God's Word tell you about how you are to remain faithful to Him and loving to your neighbor during these times?

DAY 3: THE PROMISED SAVIOR IS BORN

> But you, O Bethlehem Ephrathah, who are too little to be among the clans of Judah, from you shall come forth for Me one who is to be ruler in Israel, whose coming forth is from of old, from ancient days. (MICAH 5:2)

Finally, the time came for God's great promise, first made in the Garden of Eden and awaited by successive generations throughout history, to be fulfilled. To be mankind's Savior, the Son of God became human. As true God and true man, the Savior could keep God's commandments perfectly in our place and suffer death as our substitute. God chose a virgin named Mary, a descendant of David, from the northern town of Nazareth, to be the human mother of His Son. Jesus was conceived in Mary by the Holy Spirit's power.

Through the prophet Micah, God had given a prophecy that the Christ would come not only from David's line but also from his hometown of Bethlehem. To move Mary from Nazareth in the northern province of Galilee to Bethlehem in the southern province of Judea, God worked through Caesar Augustus, who decreed a census of the entire Roman world. In Israel, that meant returning to one's ancestral hometown, which for Mary and other descendants of David was Bethlehem.

Mary traveled there with her betrothed husband, Joseph, who was also of the royal bloodline of David, and there she gave birth to Jesus, the Savior. He is the ultimate fulfillment of God's promises throughout history, both God and man, the One who would crush the power of Satan and defeat death for God's people. Though He is all these things, He also chose to enter into human history, being born and raised in humility, experiencing what humans experience yet without sin. In Him, we have a God who shares and understands our human condition and cares deeply for the hopeless and the lost. He calls us to Himself through the Holy Spirit, and through faith in Him, we never need to fear Satan or death as we are His forever.

REFLECTION: In Jesus, God took on human flesh. What does this tell you about what God thinks of humanity? How is that significant to you as you not only live each day as God's redeemed child in Christ but also as you live your life among your fellow human creatures?

DAY 4: JESUS' CHILDHOOD

[Jesus said to Mary and Joseph,] "Why were you looking for Me? Did you not know that I must be in My Father's house?" (LUKE 2:49)

When Jesus was born, God placed a star in the sky, which was seen by the Wise Men, or magi, a group of educated scholars and magicians who had served as advisors to the Persian kings from even before Daniel's day. They followed this star westward until they reached Jerusalem, where King Herod was ruling.

When they asked where the King of the Jews was and explained how they followed His star, King Herod was stirred up with jealousy at a rival, upstart king. He learned from the Jewish priests that the Christ was prophesied to be born in Bethlehem, and Herod told the Wise Men to go and worship Him, then return and send him word where the Child was so he could also go and worship Him—intending to kill this young rival.

The Wise Men travelled to where Jesus was, at that time a young boy with His parents. After the Wise Men found the house, revered Jesus, and gave Him their gifts, they were warned in a dream not to return to Herod. When Herod learned he had been outsmarted, he ordered all the boys two years old and under in Bethlehem to be slaughtered, thinking he could do away with the rival king in his dragnet. But in a dream, an angel warned Joseph to flee to Egypt, so he left in the night with Mary and Jesus and escaped Herod.

After Herod died, Joseph planned on returning to Judea and likely to Bethlehem. But after learning Herod's son was ruling in his place, he feared to return to Bethlehem. Being warned in a dream, he took Mary and Jesus to her hometown of Nazareth, where Jesus was raised. That is why He is known as Jesus of Nazareth and not Jesus of Bethlehem.

After that, we read only one event from Jesus' childhood—when He was twelve years old and He and His family travelled to Jerusalem to celebrate the Passover. After the festival, His family returned home, but He remained in the temple courts listening to the Jewish teachers and asking them questions. Mary and Joseph searched frantically for Him for three days. When they finally found Him, Jesus told them, "Did you not know I would have to be in My Father's house?" After this, Jesus went with them and was obedient to them. He worked with Joseph as a carpenter, developing His carpentry skills and a good reputation over the following years.

REFLECTION: From what you've learned about God's plan of salvation so far, what are some important connections you can make between what God's people experienced in the past and what Jesus experienced in these early episodes of His life? Why do you suppose these connections are so important?

DAY 5: JOHN THE BAPTIST

As the people were in expectation, and all were questioning in their hearts concerning John, whether he might be the Christ, John answered them all, saying, "I baptize you with water, but He who is mightier than I is coming, the strap of whose sandals I am not worthy to untie. He will baptize you with the Holy Spirit and fire." (LUKE 3:15–16)

Malachi, the final prophet of the Old Testament who had prophesied of Jesus' coming, had also foretold a forerunner who would be like Elijah, the great prophet. For this role, God raised up John, the son of the priest Zechariah and his wife, Elizabeth, who was a cousin of Mary.

Zechariah and Elizabeth were both elderly, like Abraham and Sarah. Like Sarah, Elizabeth was unable to have children and past the age of childbirth. An angel appeared to Zechariah, just like God had appeared to Abraham and Sarah, and told him they would have a son. But just like with Abraham and Sarah, Zechariah doubted. In spite of his doubt, by God's power Elizabeth conceived. Mary was pregnant with Jesus at the same time as Elizabeth was pregnant. After receiving the news from the angel that she would be the mother of the Messiah, Mary went to visit Elizabeth, her cousin. When the two women met, Elizabeth's unborn child leapt for joy in her womb. Even before he was born, he was filled with the Holy Spirit and excited for the coming of the Messiah. When the child was born, Zechariah and Elizabeth, in line with God's command, named him John, which means "the Lord has shown favor."

John grew up and lived in the wilderness until the Holy Spirit prompted him to begin preaching a Baptism of repentance for the forgiveness of sins. John took on a similar role to Elijah, and even dressed and spoke like many of the Old Testament prophets. He confronted the hypocrisy of the leaders and prompted the people to true and faithful worship of God. John warned the people that the Messiah was living among them and would come to John to be revealed to Israel. Finally one day among the crowds of people coming to John, there stood Jesus from Nazareth. What happened next set the stage for Jesus' mission and ministry for years to come.

REFLECTION: Consider a time when God's Word really confronted and impacted you, calling you to repentance and to change a habit or an attitude. What was it? What impact did that have on your life as God's redeemed child in Christ?

Jesus Is Baptized into God's Plan

DAY 1: JESUS IS TEMPTED BY SATAN

> Again, the devil took Him to a very high mountain and showed Him all the kingdoms of the world and their glory. And he said to Him, "All these I will give You, if You will fall down and worship me." Then Jesus said to him, "Be gone, Satan! For it is written, 'You shall worship the Lord your God and Him only shall you serve.'" Then the devil left Him, and behold, angels came and were ministering to Him. (MATTHEW 4:8–11)

Jesus was baptized by John in the Jordan, bearing the sins of the world and connecting all those baptized after Him to His life, death, and resurrection. After this, Jesus began His mission in a new and special way. The Holy Spirit led Him into the wilderness where Israel had wandered forty years before entering the Promised Land. There He fasted forty days and nights, being tempted by Satan. This temptation was both the counterpart of Satan's temptation of Adam and Eve in the Garden of Eden and evocative of the temptation and refining of God's people during their wilderness wanderings. Whereas Adam and Eve were well fed, Jesus was hungry. Whereas they were in a lush garden surrounded by fruit trees, He was in a barren wilderness surrounded by rocks. But Jesus stood firm against Satan, whereas Adam and Eve quickly gave in to the temptation. Satan tempted Jesus to abuse His power and cave into thinking there was a way out of His mission to go to the cross, but Jesus stood firm in God's Word, and Satan's temptations had no power over Him. After three last temptations, Jesus commanded Satan to leave Him, and angels came and attended to His physical needs. In this, we not only see Jesus as the perfect Son of God, but we also see how He overcame Satan's temptations for us, offering His perfect life in exchange for our sinful lives.

REFLECTION: You are surrounded by temptations to sin each day, and you walk into sins daily. What does it mean to you, as God's redeemed child in Christ, that He took on the filth of your sins in His Baptism and lived a perfect life in your place?

DAY 2: JESUS CALLS THE FIRST DISCIPLES

And [Jesus] said to them, "Follow Me, and I will make you fishers of men." Immediately they left their nets and followed Him. (MATTHEW 4:19–20)

After His temptation, Jesus returned to John the Baptist and began gathering several disciples, or full-time students who would follow and learn from Him. Jesus' mission that would lead to the cross was launched in full force. He gathered His first disciples, and they returned with Him to the northern region of Israel known as Galilee. There He began to teach and gather other disciples until He had a group of twelve, specially chosen disciples. These would be eyewitnesses He would use to build His church after He had completed His earthly mission to save the world. They followed Him throughout His ministry as eyewitnesses, and through their experiences and interactions with Jesus as recorded in the Gospels, we see who the Savior is and how God's epic plan of salvation in Christ was fulfilled.

At the time they were called, these twelve men seemed unexceptional. Many of them were fishermen by trade, several were brothers, one was a hated tax collector, another a religious zealot. Though there remain many traditions about these men, from the Bible we only get limited information about their lives before and after Jesus called them to be His disciples. At the same time, in their lives and callings, we catch a glimpse of our lives as God's Church today. Though we are not called in the same special way as the Twelve, Christ has still called us outwardly unexceptional people to saving faith and a life of discipleship. Like them, we follow Jesus, listening to and abiding in His Word and bearing witness to the Gospel in our lives so that more may hear and be called to saving faith.

REFLECTION: Consider your main roles in life. What opportunities do those roles afford you to bear witness to Christ and what He has done for you through your words and actions?

DAY 3: JESUS' HEALING MIRACLES

And [Jesus] healed many who were sick with various diseases, and cast out many demons. (MARK 1:34)

Many Old Testament prophets had worked miraculous deeds by the power of the Holy Spirit, chief being Moses, Elijah, and Elisha. To establish Himself as the promised Savior, Jesus worked a multitude of miracles, especially healing miracles. It did not matter if the person was blind, deaf, lame, or crippled, Jesus was able to heal all who came to Him. It seemed like the line of people with physical needs or possessed by demons was endless, and Jesus could spend His entire ministry on earth healing the sick. He knew, however, that though this demonstration of His divine power was critical, it was not His ultimate purpose. Instead, His true mission was not to simply be a physician or exorcist but to go to the cross to be the ultimate physician of both body and soul for all time. The Old Testament prophet Isaiah described this as Jesus taking our illnesses and infirmities upon Himself even as He carried all the sins of all people from His Baptism to the cross, where He would suffer their punishment and destroy them forever.

At the same time, Jesus gave us a glimpse into what He will do on the Last Day, when He will come to restore all of God's creation—and all believers, whose bodies will be restored and made perfect and immortal forever. It is so easy for Christians to think of the end goal of faith as an eternity of spiritual life in heaven. We certainly look to this after death, and it is an amazing and wonderful gift. At the same time, we also look forward to the day when Jesus will raise the dead and God's people will live renewed, restored, sinless, and deathless lives forever in the new earth with Him.

REFLECTION: Imagine what it would be like if you and your family did not have to worry about sickness, injury, or death. How does the promise of a new creation, where Jesus will free His people from these worries forever, impact the way you think about the Christian faith today?

DAY 4: JESUS FEEDS CROWDS, DRIVES OUT DEMONS, AND RAISES THE DEAD

> Jesus said to her, "I am the resurrection and the life. Whoever believes in Me, though he die, yet shall he live, and everyone who lives and believes in Me shall never die." (JOHN 11:25–26)

Jesus in His mission and ministry demonstrated His concern and compassion for large crowds as well as individuals. One example of this was when He spent all afternoon teaching a crowd. His disciples told Him the hour was late and He should send the people away so they could find food. Instead of sending them away, Jesus directed the disciples to feed the people themselves! When they stated it was impossible, as the crowd was huge and there was no place to purchase or procure food for them, Jesus had the people sit down, gathered five loaves of bread and two fish from a young child, blessed the food, and divided it among the disciples. They distributed the food to everyone, and Jesus miraculously multiplied it, satisfying the hunger of five thousand men besides the women and children with them.

In addition, as His ministry progressed, Jesus extended His ongoing victory over Satan and his fallen angels by freeing people who were possessed by demons. With a command, Jesus drove out the demons, forcing them to obey their mighty Creator. Jesus demonstrated His supreme, divine authority over the visible and invisible, the natural and supernatural, all through the power of His Word.

Jesus even demonstrated His power over death by raising the dead. The four Gospels give us three accounts of dead people whom He raised to life—the twelve-year-old daughter of a synagogue ruler named Jairus; the only son of a widow from the town of Nain; and Lazarus, the brother of Martha and Mary, who were all dear friends of Jesus. Again, Jesus gave us a glimpse of the Last Day, when He will raise all the dead—both believers and unbelievers—and judge all mankind. Though the victory for His people was begun and assured at the cross, Jesus will crush the power of sin, death, and the devil once and for all at the final resurrection and restoration of creation.

REFLECTION: What is one blessing God has given you that you often overlook? Say a special prayer of thanks today, and pray that God would not only lead you to greater gratitude for this day but also to eager anticipation of the day when all things will be made new in the new creation and we will have no more physical needs.

DAY 5: JESUS' MIRACLES IN CREATION

> **And when they got into the boat, the wind ceased. And those in the boat worshiped Him, saying, "Truly You are the Son of God."** (MATTHEW 14:32–33)

Jesus even showed His power over His creation several times. Many of these examples occurred around the Sea of Galilee, the home base of Jesus and His disciples. At least twice He instructed His disciples, most of whom were fishermen, to throw their nets over the side of the boat for a catch of fish. Though they had fished unsuccessfully through the previous night, at Jesus' command, their nets were full of fish, breaking under the magnitude of the catch.

Another time, as Jesus and His disciples travelled across the sea, Jesus fell asleep in the stern. But as He slept, a violent storm arose on the sea. The boat filled with water. When His disciples awakened Him, He rose and commanded the winds to be quiet and the waves to be still. Miraculously, the wind and waves obeyed Him, stopping and growing instantly calm. Jesus demonstrated His power as Creator over the elements He had created.

In yet another instance, Jesus sent His disciples across the sea by boat while He remained to dismiss a gathered crowd and to pray. In the middle of the night while they travelled against the wind, the disciples saw a figure walking across the water toward them. At first, the disciples thought it was a ghost, and they cried out in fear. Jesus, however, called out to them not to worry, that it was Him. Peter, one of the Twelve, asked for Jesus to permit him to walk to Him on the water, and Jesus commanded him to come. Peter stepped down and began walking on the water to Jesus. This would not last as Peter, filled with fear, began to sink, crying out for Jesus to save Him. Jesus reached out and took Peter's hand and pulled him back onto the surface. As Jesus entered the boat, immediately the wind and waves grew calm again.

In all these things, the miracles remind us again of Christ's power to control creation for our benefit and of His promise to restore it and remove death from it forever when He returns on the Last Day.

REFLECTION: How much anxiety do natural events and natural disasters cause in the world and in your life? When Jesus makes all things new, these forces, now broken by sin, will be remade and restored. Say a prayer of thanks to Jesus, who has promised a renewed creation one day for His people.

Jesus Preaches
the Kingdom of Heaven

DAY 1: JESUS SEEKS THE LOST SHEEP OF ISRAEL

[Jesus] answered, "I was sent only to the lost sheep of the house of Israel."
(MATTHEW 15:24)

During the four hundred years between the close of the Old Testament and the coming of the Christ, the Jewish people and their religious leaders fell into some bad spiritual habits. In fact, they had completely lost their way to God. That is why Jesus said, "I was sent only to the lost sheep of the house of Israel" (Matthew 15:24).

One problem they had was thinking that doing good works and keeping the rules made a person right before God. They struggled to obey Jewish traditions and disregarded the Commandments God gave, which show we are powerless to escape our sin and we can only be saved through the promised Savior, Jesus.

Another problem for many of them was judging people by the circumstances of their lives. If a person was poor, sick, or suffering, many Jews took that as clear evidence God was punishing them for sin, while a person who enjoyed good health, riches, or popularity was considered clearly blessed by God and rewarded for his upright living. This would later cause many Jews to reject Jesus as the promised Savior because they misconstrued His crucifixion as proof He was a sinner.

During this time, the Jews also put a great deal of confidence in their ancestry. That is why John the Baptist said, "Do not presume to say to yourselves, 'We have Abraham as our father,' for I tell you, God is able from these stones to raise up children for Abraham" (Matthew 3:9).

Jesus and His forerunner, John the Baptist, were sent to God's people to expose their sin, then bring them the good news that God has kept His wonderful promise and sent the Savior to take those sins away. God's goal for His people Israel was the same in Jesus' day as it was in Abraham's, to form a nation of believers who would share God's love in Christ with all other nations. Like the Jews, we, too, can look in all the wrong places to seek God's favor. Thanks be to God that He is faithful to send a Savior even when we are unfaithful to Him!

REFLECTION: Looking at the world around you, what are the ways religious people seem to put their confidence in the wrong places? How is Christ and His free gift of salvation for you so much greater?

DAY 2: THE SERMON ON THE MOUNT

[Jesus said,] "Everyone then who hears these words of mine and does them will be like a wise man who built his house on the rock. And the rain fell, and the floods came, and the winds blew and beat on that house, but it did not fall, because it had been founded on the rock." (MATTHEW 7:24–25)

Along with all the miracles Jesus performed, He taught the individuals and crowds that came to Him. In fact, the writer Matthew took three whole chapters in his Gospel to share a sermon Jesus once preached on a mountain overlooking the Sea of Galilee. It is often known as the Sermon on the Mount.

Jesus began with eight sayings called the Beatitudes, which is the Latin word for "blessed or happy." Jesus countered the belief among Jews of His day that God grants success, like material blessings and property, to those who please Him. The Beatitudes, instead, describe the struggles and difficulties when we recognize our guilt and sin and then suffer mistreatment from others because we trust in Jesus as our Savior. Jesus promised great blessings to God's people, especially when He returns and restores God's creation.

Jesus also taught other critical truths in the sermon. He explained how to truly understand the Ten Commandments. These teach us that no matter how hard we try, we fall short of earning God's favor, for the only way we will escape God's wrath and share eternity with Him is through the merits of our Savior.

Jesus also addressed the worldly concerns that so often preoccupy our time and attention. He pointed to the beautifully adorned weeds of the field and well-fed birds of the air to remind us that just as our heavenly Father provides for them, so we can stop being anxious and trust Him to provide for us. Jesus redirected our focus to the kingdom of heaven, or the reign of Jesus as king in our lives, by assuring us He will faithfully provide for all our other needs.

REFLECTION: In what ways have you made idols of good things with which God has blessed you (success, wealth, relationships, etc.)? What are the greatest blessings Jesus actually has given you instead?

DAY 3: JESUS' PARABLES

[Jesus said,] "This is why I speak to them in parables, because seeing they do not see, and hearing they do not hear, nor do they understand. . . . But blessed are your eyes, for they see, and your ears, for they hear." (MATTHEW 13:13, 16)

Jesus was a fascinating teacher—as we might expect the Son of God to be. He used a special kind of teaching called parables. Parables are heavenly truths wrapped up in earthly stories. During His ministry, many people completely misunderstood what the kingdom of God was. As the lost sheep whom Jesus references, the people thought the promised Savior would establish the kingdom of God on earth. They did not understand that He had come to suffer and die for our sins and that only when He returned on Judgment Day would He establish God's kingdom in the new heavens and the new earth.

The impact of Jesus' parables came from the compelling stories and characters He used. As He shared fascinating images and stories, His hearers remembered and pondered them, even if they struggled to understand what Jesus was really talking about. Some parables exposed the sinfulness of the self-righteous and proud. Some parables demonstrated the amazing love God has for us worthless sinners. In one famous parable, known as the Prodigal Son, Jesus told of a father's younger son who asked for his inheritance from his father, squandered it on excessive living, then in great poverty and humility came back to beg to be treated like a servant. In a surprising twist, his father ran to embrace him, accepted him back as his son, and killed the fattened calf for a great festival of rejoicing. Meanwhile, his older brother stood out in the field, refusing to join the festivities because he thought his father should have disowned his younger son instead. The same father came out to urge the older son to really know his father's heart and join him in welcoming back his brother. This painted a picture of God's heart for the lost, as well as how His people should think of those whom God calls to Himself through Christ. Overall, Jesus' parables speak into our daily lives and vocations, revealing who God is, what He has done for us, and how we are to perceive reality as His people.

REFLECTION: If you can, recall parables of Jesus or look up a list. Which one is your favorite or most memorable parable? Why did you choose it?

DAY 4: JESUS TEACHES US HOW TO PRAY

[Jesus said,] "And when you pray, do not heap up empty phrases as the Gentiles do, for they think that they will be heard for their many words. Do not be like them, for your Father knows what you need before you ask Him." (MATTHEW 6:7–8)

Jesus also taught us how to pray. Many think God requires eloquent, powerful prayers, but Jesus taught us to pray to God as little children approach their father. In regard to prayer, Jesus reminded us that God our Father already knows what we need before we ask. This helps us understand that prayer is not revealing something to God that He was not otherwise aware of but is deepening our trust toward God and our dependence upon Him. Jesus also taught us to be confident when we pray because God promises to answer all our prayers offered through Him. This is not a promise that God will always give us the things for which we ask—but He will use His Fatherly, divine wisdom to answer and give us what we need the most, even if it does not feel like it at the time.

In Scripture, Jesus taught a specific prayer, what we call the Lord's Prayer, to His disciples. It includes praise and prayers for God's kingdom, for our earthly needs, for forgiveness and the power to forgive others, and for protection from Satan and all evil. It is a prayer that applies to every circumstance we can ever find ourselves in. The Lord's Prayer has served as a kind of battle cry of faith for God's people through the millennia, as in it we pray that God would change our will to be like His and help us to commend our lives to His care as we face the assaults of the devil, the world, and our sinful flesh. It also serves as a model for prayer so that God's people through the ages can craft their personal prayers to reflect God's heart for us.

REFLECTION: What does each line of the Lord's Prayer mean? How might you summarize each line in your own words? Why would you say it that way?

DAY 5: JESUS' LAST SUPPER

Now as they were eating, Jesus took bread, and after blessing it broke it and gave it to the disciples, and said, "Take, eat; this is My body." And He took a cup, and when He had given thanks He gave it to them, saying, "Drink of it, all of you, for this is My blood of the covenant, which is poured out for many for the forgiveness of sins." (MATTHEW 26:26–28)

Jesus' final teachings before His crucifixion were for His followers, primarily His twelve disciples. He gathered with them the night before He died as they celebrated the Passover feast, His Last Supper with them. At that Passover supper, an argument broke out among the Twelve regarding which of them would be the greatest when Jesus came into His kingdom. Instead of chastising them for their selfishness, Jesus got up from the table, wrapped a towel around His waist, and began washing their feet one by one in the manner of a servant washing the dirty feet of houseguests. When He was finished, He taught them that in His kingdom the greatest will humble themselves to serve others as He was humbling Himself to serve them.

Jesus then predicted the two sins His close disciples would commit against Him. The first concerned Judas Iscariot, who would betray Jesus to the Jewish leaders for a meager sum of thirty silver pieces. Then there was Peter, the one who had seemed strongest and most loyal of the Twelve. Jesus predicted that Peter would deny knowing Jesus that night and that he would do it three times. Jesus also pointed out that all the disciples would flee from Him and go into hiding that very same night.

Jesus then instituted the Lord's Supper to give all His followers a way to not only remember His suffering and death for their salvation but also to receive His very body and blood. In the meal, which is to continue when God's people gather until Jesus returns, His people receive the very body He gave into death as a sacrifice for their sins and the blood He shed as their Passover Lamb. Just as the blood of the Passover lamb protected the firstborn Israelites in Egypt, this blood of the new covenant protects God's people from death and eternal damnation on Judgment Day.

REFLECTION: What events and words from the history of God's people come to mind when considering Jesus' final teachings to His disciples? Why do you think they matter so much?

God's Plan of Salvation Completed

> And [Jesus] withdrew from them about a stone's throw, and knelt down and prayed, saying, "Father, if You are willing, remove this cup from Me. Nevertheless, not My will, but Yours, be done." (LUKE 22:41–42)

After Jesus finished His Passover meal with His disciples, He led them out to the Mount of Olives into a section called the Garden of Gethsemane. There He left all but three, Peter, James, and John, whom He brought along with Him to a certain place to pray. There, Jesus pleaded with them to watch with Him and pray, then He went out a bit further on and began to pray earnestly.

He pleaded with His Father to take away the cup of suffering laid before Him. The bitter cup Jesus was to drink was the wrath of God on all human sins—which for us would be suffering in hell forever without end. In His mission, Jesus alone could bear God's wrath, being utterly forsaken by God His Father. Jesus asked the Father to take away the cup, to find another way to save humanity—then yielded up His will saying, "Not My will but Your will be done." What a great model for our prayers! It is fine to express our will to God, to state the resolution we would like to see. However, we, too, need to humble ourselves, recognize our Father's superior, loving wisdom, and yield to His perfect will.

Jesus taught us how to pray, especially in those times when praying is hardest because we are confronted with monumental pain and challenges in life. We find comfort in this prayer, especially when we are afraid to let our thoughts go where circumstances are leading them, or when our feelings of grief, pain, or fear are so great we are afraid to plunge into them and would rather live in denial. Jesus knew only His Father could prepare and strengthen Him for the terrible ordeal awaiting Him—just as He alone can help us through the hardest things in our lives—including the hour of death.

REFLECTION: What is one thing out of your control that is bringing you anxiety or stress right now? Pray that God would strengthen your faith and trust in Him during this time, knowing that Jesus has already endured the eternal suffering for this lost and broken humanity.

DAY 2: JESUS' TRIAL BEFORE THE JEWS

[The council said,] "If You are the Christ, tell us." But [Jesus] said to them, "If I tell you, you will not believe, and if I ask you, you will not answer. But from now on the Son of Man shall be seated at the right hand of the power of God." (LUKE 22:67–69)

Jesus had just finished praying and was waking His disciples when a great crowd of soldiers, guards, and priests entered the garden led by Judas, the betrayer. Judas identified Jesus with a kiss of greeting, and in a moment of rage, Peter took out his sword and swung it at one of the mob, cutting off a man's ear. At this, Jesus commanded Peter to put the sword back in its sheath and miraculously healed the man's ear. Even so, the guards seized Jesus, bound Him, and led Him back into the city to the high priest's house. Jesus' disciples fled into the night in terror for their own lives, just as Jesus had said they would.

During Jesus' nighttime trial before the Jewish leaders, He was questioned about many things but kept silent. False witnesses were brought in to testify against Him, but their testimony did not agree, which was a requirement for the death penalty according to Moses' law. Finally, the high priest put Jesus under oath, asking if He was God's Son. Jesus answered that He was and that they would see Him coming on the clouds of glory on the Last Day. At this, the leaders condemned Him for blasphemy, or claiming to be God's Son, and they took turns beating Him. They then led Him off to Pilate, the Roman governor over that area.

As this trial went on, Peter stood outside with the guards trying to learn what was happening to Jesus. Servant girls began asking if he was with Jesus. He was asked three times, and three times Peter denied any knowledge of Jesus or association with Him. Then the rooster crowed twice, and at that moment, Peter saw Jesus looking at him and remembered Jesus' prediction at the Last Supper. Peter broke down and wept bitterly at his failure and guilt. He, like all of humanity, is guilty of denying God and in need of undeserved forgiveness.

REFLECTION: What are ways that you or your household deny or hide your faith out in the world? What is one thing you can do to change that pattern and more joyfully embrace your Christian identity in the world?

DAY 3: JESUS' TRIAL BEFORE PILATE

> Then Pilate said to Him, "So You are a king?" Jesus answered, "You say that I am a king. For this purpose I was born and for this purpose I have come into the world—to bear witness to the truth. Everyone who is of the truth listens to My voice." (JOHN 18:37)

The Jewish priests brought Jesus before Pilate, the main Roman official for the area, and accused Him of three capital crimes: causing an insurrection, teaching that taxes should not be paid to the emperor, and claiming to be a king. Pilate, seeing through the politics of the religious leaders, did not even investigate the first two charges, knowing they were false. He did question Jesus, however, about His kingship. When Jesus assured Pilate that He is a king but His kingdom is not of this world, Pilate announced that there were no grounds for a charge against Jesus. Pilate should have released Jesus at that point. Because Pilate feared the religious leaders, he did not use his power to do so. Instead, he tried some tricks to get the Jewish priests to agree to free Jesus.

Pilate had a custom of giving the Passover crowd the choice between two criminals, one of whom he would release. Usually these were political prisoners who had spoken up against Rome, not dangerous criminals. But this time, he took the worst prisoner he had—Barabbas, who had committed murder in an insurrection and was possibly the one intended to be executed on that middle cross that day—and offered him up against Jesus. Pilate badly underestimated how dangerous the priests considered Jesus and was shocked when they persuaded the crowds to call for Barabbas to be released and Jesus to be crucified.

Pilate's last gamble was to have Jesus brutally flogged, an act that often left victims crippled for life, hoping the Jewish leaders would be satisfied that Jesus suffered enough and was no longer a threat to them. When this did not work, Pilate, to avoid a riot, consented to their demand and sentenced Jesus to death by crucifixion. Jesus, bombarded by cries of hate and beaten to the point of death, still humbly and willingly went to the cross for the sins of all people, including the very people who hated Him.

REFLECTION: What teachings of Jesus do people today have a hard time accepting or even plainly reject? How do Jesus' words and actions here reflect His heart toward those people?

THE TREE OF LIFE: GOD'S PROMISE OF SALVATION

DAY 4: JESUS IS CRUCIFIED

> And when they came to the place that is called The Skull, there they crucified Him, and the criminals, one on His right and one on His left. And Jesus said, "Father, forgive them, for they know not what they do." (LUKE 23:33–34)

The Roman soldiers mocked Jesus as King of the Jews, weaving a crown of thorns and putting it on His head. They put a purple robe around His torn shoulders and knelt in mockery before Him, slapping Him, spitting on Him, and mocking Him.

As they led Jesus and the other two criminals out to be crucified, Jesus' strength gave out and He fell under the weight of the cross. Since Jesus was too weak to carry it, they compelled a watcher named Simon from Cyrene to carry it for Him. Finally, when they reached the place of execution, a hill named Golgotha outside the city walls, they crucified Him.

During Jesus' first three hours on the cross, from around nine in the morning to noon, daylight illuminated the scene. Rings of people stood around the cross watching Jesus, and those along the road going into Jerusalem mocked Him as a fraud. Priests mocked Jesus, whose name means "the Lord saves," by stating, "He saved others, but He can't save Himself. Let Him come down from the cross, and we will believe in Him." In response to all this, Jesus prayed, "Father, forgive them, for they know not what they do." This prayer echoes through time, pleading to God to also forgive the many sins we commit against Him, sins for which Jesus suffered and died.

The two thieves crucified on either side of Jesus also mocked Him for a time. Eventually, one of the criminals was brought to repentance and faith. This criminal rebuked the other, asking the other criminal if he feared God. He pointed out that they were receiving the just punishment for their deeds, but Jesus had done nothing wrong. He then asked Jesus to remember him when Jesus came into His kingdom, to which Jesus promised, "Truly I say to you, today you will be with Me in paradise." In this scene, we see both God's wrath for sinful humanity being poured out on Christ and His mercy forgiving those who believe in Him.

REFLECTION: Take some serious time today to reflect on your sins and your need for forgiveness, asking God in Christ to forgive your many sins. Then go about your day rejoicing in the forgiveness that is yours in Christ, which nothing can take away.

DAY 5: JESUS DIES

> Then Jesus, calling out with a loud voice, said, "Father, into Your hands I commit My spirit!" And having said this He breathed His last. (LUKE 23:46)

At noon, while Jesus was dying on the cross, the sun stopped shining and darkness fell over the land. Three hours later, at the ninth hour (three o'clock in the afternoon), Jesus called out in a heartbreaking voice, "My God, My God, why have You forsaken Me?" Here was hell itself for all to see. Jesus was forsaken by God the Father, suffering unbearable agony with no relief, with no respite. Hell is not a place of partying as some dream, but lonely isolation and lingering pain. Yet Jesus remained on the cross for us, suffering all that to offer us forgiveness, life, and salvation.

At the ninth hour, Jesus' punishment was complete, and the Father was satisfied that the punishment for all our sins had been paid in full. The Gospel writer John tells us, "After this, Jesus, knowing that all was now finished, said (to fulfill the Scripture), 'I thirst.' . . . When Jesus had received sour wine, He said, 'It is finished.'" (John 19:28, 30). All His sufferings were completed; our debt to God the Father had been completely paid. There is nothing we need to do but believe it by the power of the Holy Spirit. Then Jesus prayed, "Father, into Your hands I commit My spirit" (Luke 23:46). He yielded up His spirit and breathed His last. In these final words, we see how Jesus' perfect relationship with His Father had been restored. He was no longer forsaken. His mission was completed.

At this, the curtain of the temple was supernaturally torn in two, indicating that in Jesus' death, the dividing wall between God and man was removed and some of the dead in the city miraculously rose to new life, a taste of the gift Jesus will give to all His people when He returns on the Last Day and raises all the dead.

Jesus was then buried in a tomb by two secret disciples who were members of the Jewish high court. Pilate gave them permission, the tomb was sealed, and a guard was set in an attempt to prevent any tampering with the body.

REFLECTION: Take some time to ponder the great gift Jesus has given you—suffering the punishment of hell in your place and giving you eternal life in its place. Then, offer a prayer of thanks for this wonderful gift.

Jesus Conquers Death

DAY 1: JESUS IS RISEN FROM THE DEAD

> Now on the first day of the week Mary Magdalene came to the tomb early, while it was still dark, and saw that the stone had been taken away from the tomb. So she ran and went to Simon Peter and the other disciple, the one whom Jesus loved. (JOHN 20:1–2)

Jesus' resurrection from the dead opens a new day for all descendants of Adam and Eve. The snare of Satan is broken, death has lost its sting and its hold over all humanity. The resurrection gives us the assurance that our graves will not be our final resting places. Just as Christ arose from the dead, we, too, will rise to new life with Him in the new heavens and the new earth as He calls us forth from our graves to live with Him in paradise forever.

Interestingly, there were no eyewitnesses the moment Jesus rose. Witnesses only saw the aftereffects of that resurrection. It began with the stone rolled away from the tomb and continued with the empty grave cloths lying in the same place they had been when Jesus' body was still within them, with the head cloth nearby, neatly folded.

Mary Magdalene, one of Jesus' followers, saw the empty tomb and ran back to inform the disciples. When she returned to town, she told Peter and John someone had taken Jesus' body. The two disciples ran out to see for themselves, and sure enough, the grave was open, and the linen and spices were lying empty right where Jesus' body had been. The two male disciples returned home, wondering about the things they had seen.

Mary, who had returned to the tomb by this time, stayed there weeping, convinced someone had removed Jesus' body. First, two angels appeared to Mary, and then Jesus Himself. When Jesus spoke her name, suddenly the sorrow lifted for Mary, and in wonder, amazement, and recognition, Mary cried out, "Rabboni!" which means "Teacher." She knew Jesus was risen and alive. She grabbed hold of Him, intent on never letting go. Jesus told her not to cling to Him but to go and tell His brothers that He was risen from the dead. So Mary rushed back with the good news, "I have seen the Lord!"

REFLECTION: In Baptism, we are connected with Christ's death and resurrection so that, though we will die, we who are baptized, like Christ, will one day be raised to new life. What makes this promise so remarkable to you?

DAY 2: ON THE ROAD TO EMMAUS

> **And beginning with Moses and all the Prophets, [Jesus] interpreted to them in all the Scriptures the things concerning Himself.** (LUKE 24:27)

Mary Magdalene went back and told Jesus' followers in hiding about His resurrection, but the men did not believe her. Two men, not numbered among Jesus' chosen Twelve, decided to get out of Jerusalem while they could.

As they walked along, they spoke to each other about the whirlwind of things that had happened in Jerusalem, including Jesus' triumphant entry, His popularity among the crowds, His arrest, trials, and crucifixion. And now they also talked about the empty tomb and Mary's report. They had no hope or optimism. They had had many hopes and dreams about Jesus of Nazareth, particularly that He would redeem Israel from the hated Romans. Now their dreams were as dead as, they supposed, Jesus.

Then a stranger approached them on the road and noticed how dejected they looked, their faces downcast. He asked what they were talking about, and their response was shock and surprise. The stranger patiently listened as they reported about all that had happened with Jesus, giving them the chance to express their disappointment. After this, the stranger told them, "O foolish ones, and slow of heart to believe all that the prophets have spoken! Was it not necessary that the Christ should suffer these things and enter into His glory?" And then the stranger, Jesus Himself, led them through the Scriptures, as we did in the previous weeks of these ten weeks, and "interpreted to them in all the Scriptures the things concerning Himself" (Luke 24:25–27).

Finally at their destination, the stranger joined the two men for dinner. He took the dinner bread, gave thanks, broke it, gave it to them, and suddenly they recognized it was Jesus. Jesus then miraculously vanished from their midst! The two men immediately got up and rushed back into Jerusalem! They shared with each other how their hearts burned within them as He talked with them, opening up everything in the Old Testament that had been written about Him. They finally reached the upper room where most of the Twelve were gathered and told them how Jesus had revealed Himself to them along the road.

REFLECTION: What does Jesus' interaction with the two men reveal to you about both His mission and His caring attitude toward common people?

DAY 3: JESUS MEETS THOMAS'S UNBELIEF

> Thomas answered Him, "My Lord and my God!" Jesus said to him, "Have you believed because you have seen Me? Blessed are those who have not seen and yet have believed." (JOHN 20:28–29)

The two men from the Emmaus road burst into the upper room where the disciples were gathered, and they all stood together talking. Suddenly Jesus appeared, right in the midst of them! Frightened, they immediately assumed He was a ghost, a logical conclusion since He hadn't knocked on the locked door or climbed through a window; He just materialized out of thin air.

Jesus dispelled their fears by having them touch Him to see He had flesh and bones, which spirits do not have. He also ate some fish to prove He was not a spirit, for if a mere spirit tried to eat fish, the food would just fall to the floor.

After sharing God's peace with them, Jesus did something amazing. He breathed on them to give them the Holy Spirit, and in so doing gave them the power to forgive sins or withhold forgiveness. Already, just hours after His resurrection, Jesus was forming and establishing His Church through which He continues His forgiving work after His ascension into heaven.

Thomas, one of the Twelve, was absent at that time. When he later heard of what had happened, he refused to believe the testimony of the others who had seen Jesus. He insisted on seeing Jesus for himself, putting his fingers in the nail scars in Jesus' hands and putting his hand into the spear mark in Jesus' side. His refusal to believe was not merely that he required physical proof but that the thought of Jesus' resurrection was so preposterous to him that without God's intervention, he would never believe it.

A week later, Jesus appeared to the disciples again in the same place, but this time, Thomas was present. Jesus revealed Himself specifically to Thomas, who confessed his faith in Jesus as both Lord and God. Jesus said, "Have you believed because you have seen Me? Blessed are those who have not seen and yet have believed" (John 20:29). We, who hear God's Word and believe today, are truly blessed with the gift of faith!

REFLECTION: Thomas usually gets a bad reputation as a "doubter," but we all experience doubts about our faith. In fact, none of us would have saving faith without the Holy Spirit working through the Means of Grace. Say a prayer thanking God for the gift of faith, which we would never have without the Holy Spirit.

DAY 4: JESUS REINSTATES PETER

And Jesus came and said to them, "All authority in heaven and on earth has been given to Me. Go therefore and make disciples of all nations, baptizing them in the name of the Father and of the Son and of the Holy Spirit, teaching them to observe all that I have commanded you. And behold, I am with you always, to the end of the age." (MATTHEW 28:18–20)

After the Passover and Feast of Unleavened Bread were over, the disciples returned from Jerusalem to Galilee. Peter said he was going fishing, and a group of them joined him. They spent all night fishing but caught nothing. In the morning, they saw a stranger on the shore who asked if they had caught any fish. Hearing they had not, He instructed them to throw their nets on the other side of the boat. When they did, they caught so many their nets began breaking and their two boats could not hold all the fish without starting to sink. The disciple John recognized it was Jesus. When Peter heard, he jumped overboard and hastily swam in to meet Jesus. The other disciples followed, hauling the boats full of fish to shore.

After their breakfast with Him, Jesus asked Peter three times, "Do you love Me?" Peter assured Him of his love each time. Jesus was bringing Peter back to his three denials during Jesus' Jewish trials, and Peter was deeply hurt the third time Jesus questioned his love. Jesus then prophesied that Peter would die by crucifixion, giving the assurance that by that kind of death, Peter would be faithful to Jesus when later asked to confess if he was Jesus' follower.

Then on another occasion, Jesus gathered many believers on a mountain in Galilee and gave them the Great Commission to go and make disciples of all nations by baptizing them—in the name of the Father, Son, and Holy Spirit—and teaching them to observe all that Jesus had commanded them. Jesus continued preparing and equipping His Church for their life and mission after His ascension.

REFLECTION: The Christian life, as God's redeemed child, is one of constantly living in our baptismal identities and continually learning to observe and follow Jesus' teaching. What is one way you can more carefully and intentionally be in God's Word and prayer in your life?

DAY 5: JESUS ASCENDS TO HEAVEN

[Jesus said,] "But you will receive power when the Holy Spirit has come upon you, and you will be My witnesses in Jerusalem and in all Judea and Samaria, and to the end of the earth." And when He had said these things, as they were looking on, He was lifted up, and a cloud took Him out of their sight. (ACTS 1:8–9)

Jesus appeared to His disciples in many places and many ways during the forty days after His resurrection. The disciples would eventually all go through severe trials, and tradition tells us most were martyred for the faith. Clearly, they were so convinced by these resurrection appearances that Jesus was truly risen that they held firm to their faith, even unto death, by the power of the Holy Spirit.

Jesus met the disciples again in Jerusalem on the fortieth day. He had been revealing Himself to many different people, sharing the good news of His resurrection with them. Now He led them out to the Mount of Olives, a hill outside Jerusalem. While He was blessing them, He rose up into the sky, and a cloud hid Him from their sight. While they looked up, an angel appeared and told them that Jesus would return the same way they saw Him go.

Jesus entered, or ascended, into the heavenly places and took His seat at the right hand of the Father. Like Joseph at the right hand of Pharaoh or Daniel at the right hand of Darius, Jesus governs all things that happen in God's kingdom—creation—until the day He will return to judge the living and dead and restore all creation and all of us believers. Though He is at the right hand of God, He is still present with His people, just as He had promised. He works through the Means of Grace, the Word and Sacraments, which He gives to His Church to call people to faith, granting them forgiveness, eternal life, and salvation.

REFLECTION: From everything you have learned so far about the Christian faith and the narrative of salvation, what is so significant about Jesus sitting on His throne at the right hand of the Father? What does that mean for God's people today? What does it mean for you personally?

The End of Our Story

DAY 1: THE GREAT FLOOD

> [Jesus said,] "Therefore, stay awake, for you do not know on what day your Lord is coming." (MATTHEW 24:42)

What will Judgment Day look like when Christ returns? The Bible gives us some hints. During this final week of reflections, we will first look at judgment, then the resurrection to eternal life.

The Old Testament describes three events when God judged the world—in each, He punished the ungodly and saved the believers. We begin with the great flood recorded in Genesis 6–8. Since the flood during the time of Noah was worldwide and every mountain under the sky was covered by over twenty feet of water (Genesis 7:20), there was no escaping God's judgment except inside the ark that Noah had built. So God provided a way of salvation, but only those who believed His threat of judgment were saved.

Jesus spoke about the unbelievers who were swept away in that terrible catastrophe: "They were eating and drinking and marrying and being given in marriage, until the day when Noah entered the ark, and the flood came and destroyed them all" (Luke 17:27). Consider those words carefully. That devastating flood came out of nowhere and was totally unexpected by everyone but Noah's family. The unbelievers got up that morning, lived their lives as usual, eating and drinking, marrying and being given in marriage, and suddenly the flood came, and it was too late.

But for Noah and his family, God provided a way to survive the flood—many years before He had warned Noah of the coming flood and commanded him to build the ark. The Holy Spirit gave Noah faith to believe God and obey Him. He built the gigantic ark, which saved himself, his family, and representatives of all the creatures that filled the land and air.

Jesus compared the day of the flood to the day of His return: "So will it be in the days of the Son of Man" (Luke 17:26). In other words, people will be eating and drinking, marrying and giving in marriage, going about their daily lives with the expectation that life will go on and there will be a tomorrow. But time will run out, and it will be too late. Christ will be here to judge all people. It is a call for each of us to be ready and watch for that day when Christ returns. It is also a reminder to share the warning and God's salvation in Jesus Christ with everyone we can.

REFLECTION: What do you do to prepare your household for potential threats and dangers? What can you do with your family to be watchful for the day of Christ's return?

DAY 2: THE DESTRUCTION OF SODOM

[Jesus said,] "Likewise, just as it was in the days of Lot—they were eating and drinking, buying and selling, planting and building, but on the day when Lot went out from Sodom, fire and sulfur rained from heaven and destroyed them all—so will it be on the day when the Son of Man is revealed." (LUKE 17:28–30)

Unlike Noah's worldwide flood, the second judgment we look at this week was not universal; it struck a relatively small region south of Canaan. It did, however, have an eerie similarity to how the New Testament describes Christ's return.

Abraham's nephew Lot was living as a stranger in Sodom when the Lord, having heard the cries of oppression, sent two angels into Sodom and Gomorrah to see if it was filled with violence and oppression. Lot welcomed the angels into his home. That night, the men of Sodom surrounded the house ready to do violence to the two angels who had appeared as men. The angels struck the men of the town with blindness, then led Lot and his family out of Sodom by the hand and urged them to flee quickly to the mountains:

Escape there quickly, for I can do nothing till you arrive there. (GENESIS 19:22)

What a remarkable show of God's love—His desire to save the righteous can even delay His judgment on the ungodly.

When the fire and brimstone fell upon Sodom and Gomorrah, Lot and his family were gone. But for those who remained in the city, there was no safe hiding place, no way to escape.

What Jesus had said about the time of Noah and the flood, He repeated about this horrific judgment:

Likewise, just as it was in the days of Lot—they were eating and drinking, buying and selling, planting and building, but on the day when Lot went out from Sodom, fire and sulfur rained from heaven and destroyed them all—so will it be on the day when the Son of Man is revealed. (LUKE 17:28–30)

Jesus was clear—the people of Sodom did not expect their lives to end that day. They were eating and drinking, buying with the intent to use that which they bought, selling to use the money from that sale for some purpose, and making plans for the future. But they did not live to see the sun set that day. The same will be true the day Christ returns.

REFLECTION: How do your personal plans (business, vacation, youth sports, personal time) distract you from focusing on receiving God's gifts in worship or in your household? Why do you let your priorities get so backwards?

DAY 3: THE DESTRUCTION OF JERUSALEM

> And while some were speaking of the temple, how it was adorned with noble stones and offerings, [Jesus] said, "As for these things that you see, the days will come when there will not be left here one stone upon another that will not be thrown down." (LUKE 21:5–6)

Next on the list of judgment topics is the destruction of Jerusalem. This event is a bit different than the flood of Noah's day and the destruction of Sodom and Gomorrah in Lot's. We do not have any record of Jesus comparing the past destruction of Jerusalem by the Babylonians to Judgment Day. But He did prophesy the future destruction of Jerusalem by the Romans:

> And when He drew near and saw the city, He wept over it, saying, "Would that you, even you, had known on this day the things that make for peace! But now they are hidden from your eyes. For the days will come upon you, when your enemies will set up a barricade around you and surround you and hem you in on every side and tear you down to the ground, you and your children within you. And they will not leave one stone upon another in you, because you did not know the time of your visitation." (LUKE 19:41–44)

Jesus picked up that theme later when teaching His disciples about Judgment Day. He spoke about the destruction of the temple, warning them to flee when they see the Roman legions marching on the city.

On the day Jesus returns, the angel armies will come pouring through the clouds. Then it will be too late for unbelievers to find relief and rescue in Jesus. Today is the day to sit at His feet, confess your sins, and remember His great sacrifice for you, which alone can save you from the wrath to come on sinful humanity when He returns.

REFLECTION: What is so troubling for you and others in society about the concept of a final "judgment day"? How does the work of Jesus for you on the cross transform how you view the final judgment of the living and the dead?

DAY 4: JESUS RAISES A YOUNG DAUGHTER AND AN ONLY SON

And when the Lord saw her, He had compassion on her and said to her, "Do not weep." Then He came up and touched the bier, and the bearers stood still. And He said, "Young man, I say to you, arise." And the dead man sat up and began to speak, and Jesus gave him to his mother. (LUKE 7:13–15)

Having examined three accounts of God's judgment in the Scriptures, we turn to ask what the resurrection will be like on the Last Day? Last week, we looked at Jesus' resurrection, which guarantees that we will not remain in our graves but that He will faithfully raise us to eternal life. To broaden our understanding, we now study the three times recorded in the Gospels when Jesus raised the dead to life.

One instance was a twelve-year-old daughter of a synagogue ruler named Jairus. When Jairus first approached Jesus, his daughter was dying. He desperately hoped Jesus would get to his house before his daughter would die. Along the way, however, he received word that his daughter had died and that he shouldn't bother the Teacher anymore. But Jesus responded, "Do not fear, only believe" (Mark 5:36).

Jesus reached Jairus's home and found a large number of mourners. He asked why they were making so much commotion when the girl was not dead but asleep. They laughed at Him since they thought they knew better. Jesus, though, made everyone leave the house except for the child's parents and Peter, James, and John. Then He went in to her room, took her by the hand, and said, "Little girl, I say to you, arise" (Mark 5:41). And she arose. Jesus and many New Testament writers describe death as a sleep from which Christ will awaken us on Judgment Day.

A second account came as Jesus and His disciples were walking into a town called Nain. They meet another group coming out of town—a funeral procession. Jesus saw the mother of the dead man. Knowing she was already a widow and this was her only son, His heart went out to her. He told her, "Do not weep." He touched the coffin they were carrying and said, "Young man, I say to you, arise," and immediately the young man sat up and started talking. That is the power Jesus has over death. It will be simple for Him to raise us from our graves with nothing but a word when He returns on the Last Day.

REFLECTION: Jesus mourns with those who mourn death but also talks about death as if it were as light as sleep. What does this mean for you and how you should approach others in their grief?

DAY 5: JESUS RAISES LAZARUS

> Behold, I am coming soon, bringing My recompense with Me, to repay each one for what he has done. I am the Alpha and the Omega, the first and the last, the beginning and the end. (REVELATION 22:12–13)

There is one more account in the Gospels when Jesus raised a dead person to life. It is an extremely fitting place to end this study because Jesus discussed Judgment Day with the sister of the dead man.

Before Jesus died, He received word that a good friend, Lazarus, was seriously ill. Lazarus's sisters told Jesus He needed to rush to Lazarus to heal him. When Jesus received word, however, He remained where He was two extra days. After those days, Jesus told His disciples to rise, as He was going to wake up Lazarus. They thought Lazarus was sleeping and would recover, but Jesus told them plainly that Lazarus had died and He was going there to raise him from the dead.

When Jesus came near, Lazarus' sister Martha came out to meet Him. Jesus told her, "I am the resurrection and the life. Whoever believes in Me, though he die, yet shall he live, and everyone who lives and believes in Me shall never die" (John 11:25–26). Jesus spoke both about our coming death and our resurrection on Judgment Day when He returns. When we die, only our body dies; our spirit does not die. Like the repentant thief next to Jesus on the cross, we who believe in Jesus will be with Him in paradise. Then on the Last Day when He returns, He will raise our bodies.

Then Jesus went out to the tomb where Lazarus had been dead and buried for four days. Jesus instructed the people to roll the stone blocking the tomb's entrance away. Then He prayed to His Father, and in a loud voice said, "Lazarus, come out" (John 11:43). The dead man came out, wrapped in linen cloths.

There is nothing magical about the day Christ will return. It will be a common, average, ordinary day just like every day before it. What will make it special is the return of Jesus Christ, the mighty Son of God and Savior of the world. He is the resurrection and the life. He will return with His mighty angel armies, raise all the dead—divide them into believers and unbelievers—and judge them. The unbelievers will be cast out of His creation and confined in hell forever. The glorified believers will live with Him in the new heavens and the new earth—the creation He just restored—and will enjoy paradise with Him forever. That is the narrative of the Bible, the sweep of the epic salvation story—the story of Jesus and us.

REFLECTION: What have been your biggest takeaways from reading through and thinking on God's plan of salvation? Why do you think that is?